CAMOUFLAGE

Created and Produced by Firecrest Books Ltd
in association with John Francis/Bernard Thornton Artists

Copyright © 1999 Firecrest Books Ltd
and Copyright © 1999 John Francis/Bernard Thornton Artists

Published by Tangerine Press™, an imprint of Scholastic Inc.
555 Broadway, New York, NY 10012

ISBN 0-439-09591-3

Library of Congress Cataloging-in-Publication Data

Stonehouse, Bernard.
Camouflage / Bernard Stonehouse ; illustrated by John Francis.
p. cm.
Includes index.
SUMMARY: Explains how various animals on land, in the air, and in
the water use camouflage to hide from predators or to capture
their prey.
ISBN 0-439-09591-3 (pbk.)
1. Camouflage (Biology) Juvenile literature. [1. Camouflage
(Biology)] I. Francis, John, 1950- ill. II. Title.
QL759 .S75 1999

Printed and bound in Belgium
First printing September 1999

CAMOUFLAGE

Bernard Stonehouse

Illustrated by
John Francis

TANGERINE PRESS™ and associated logo
and design are trademarks of Scholastic Inc.

For Tricia

Art and Editorial Direction by
Peter Sackett

Designed by
Paul Richards, Designers & Partners

Edited by
Norman Barrett

Color separation by
Job Color, Italy

Printed and bound by
Casterman, Belgium

Contents

— Introduction HIDE AND SEEK

A most striking feature of many animals is the way they blend with their background to deceive other animals. This is called camouflage, and it works in two main ways. It helps predators to hide from their prey — to creep up within striking distance and pounce before they are observed. And it helps prey to hide from their predators, to feed or go about their business without drawing attention to themselves, to sleep without being rudely awakened, to nest or raise their young without being seen. If they are seen, then camouflage makes them look like something else — a rock, a stick, or anything that is much less interesting to the predator.

Camouflage — the word originally meant a wisp of smoke, blown in the face to deceive — takes many forms, but is usually a visual trick, based on color or shape. Sometimes the colors are brilliant, to match a sunlit background. Sometimes they are drab, to blend with gray rocks, dull skies, or evening light. Sometimes deceptive movement is involved, sometimes complete stillness. This book shows examples of all these forms of camouflage. A few are quite simple: a white bird against snow, a dark mammal patrolling through the night. Many are more complex: a spotted fish that can change its spots to match different backgrounds, a stippled bird that exactly matches a particular background, an insect that mimics, of all unlikely things, a complex, delicately tinted orchid.

It looks like a leaf — but it is an insect. That is camouflage.

Camouflage is never completely and wholly successful. If we were all fully camouflaged, nobody would find anyone else. Mating would stop, parents would lose their young. Predators would go hungry, and prey become too numerous for their own good. But effective camouflage prolongs the life or increases the chances of success of many creatures. What astonishes naturalists is the thousands of different ways that nature has evolved to camouflage animals. This book looks at the sheer inventiveness of camouflage in animals ranging from tiny insects to large mammals.

Snow leopard AMBUSHING AN ARGALI

Snow leopards live in the mountains of Asia, often in damp cloud, usually in mist, sometimes in snow and ice. They probably evolved from lowland leopards — vividly spotted cats whose tan-and-black markings provide excellent cover in the sunlight and shadows of a tropical forest. But a lowland leopard in a mountain mist would shine like a lantern, and be miserably cold as well. So the snow leopards of central Asia have developed a much thicker, warmer coat of much subtler colors.

This one is crouching very low, on a rocky sheep track high on a mountain face. Advancing along the track is an argali, a large mountain sheep that lives in this harsh, semidesert country. It is a tense moment. The ram has spotted something odd — a strange thing on the path that was not there yesterday. He may not know it is a leopard, but he senses danger. His ears are cocked, his nostrils flaring to pick up a scent. He is poised, ready to run. The leopard's head is low, the huge muscles of its back and its hind legs hunched ready for action. If it stays absolutely still, the argali will step forward — and the strange thing on the path will turn into a blur of murderous teeth and claws.

Checkered elephant shrew SQUARES FOR SAFETY

Most shrews are mouse-sized animals with long pointed noses. They live very quietly in grassland, hunting for small insects. Elephant shrews are elephantine in three ways. First, among shrews they are enormous — up to about 1 foot (30 cm) long, with a further 6 inches (15 cm) or more of tail. Second, their noses extend like Pinocchio's into a flexible, mobile trunk, useful for sniffing out insects among dead leaves and grass. Third, they live in Africa, where the biggest elephants live.

Checkers is a game played on a board with alternate red and black squares. Checkered shrews get their name from the curious pattern of dark squares and rectangles in the paler fur along each flank. This is just another pattern of camouflage, like the tiger's stripes and the leopard's spots, that helps to make these little animals almost invisible in the undergrowth. But they have other ways of disappearing, too. Long thin legs, especially in the rear, give them an extraordinary ability to run and jump. If a hawk swoops down, they streak for home along well-known paths. If it strikes, they leap sideways and keep running, then leap again, and race off in another direction.

Ocelot BLENDING WITH THE FOREST

Here is an ocelot with a mission. It is hungry and has its eye on a fat male cock-of-the-rock. The two animals live in a damp forest in Peru, South America, and have met halfway up a tall tree. The branches are covered with mosses, orchids, and other small plants. The ocelot is as much at home aloft in the branches as down below. Its name is based on a Mexican native word meaning "field jaguar." It is a fierce hunter, about 4 feet (1.2 m) long, slender enough to climb and jump, but weighing more than three fat house cats.

The ocelot's tawny-and-black stippled coat blends beautifully with the forest background, almost well enough to fool the bird. By contrast, the cock-of-the-rock sticks out like a sore thumb. This might seem strange. But while it pays the cat not to be seen, the bird has to advertise its presence, with color, calls, and display, so that it can find a mate.

The cat gazes with eyes unblinking, flicking the tip of its tail (down there on the left) to divert the bird's attention. The bird sees the movement and watches warily — just a slight movement, nothing to worry about. The cat inches closer along the branch, helped by the sound of the wind, the rustling leaves, and the vivid contrasts of light and shade. Will it catch its prey? Not always.

Three-toed sloth A LAZY LIFE

Sloth is just another name for laziness, and the three-toed sloth is as lazy an animal as you could meet anywhere. All the seven different kinds of sloths all spend their lives hanging upside down from the branches of tropical forest trees. They hang on by their claws, which are enlarged finger- and toenails. Some kinds have three fingers and toes, some only two. This is one of the three-toed species.

Scientists who study the habits of sloths complain of boredom – sloths never do anything. Their food, mainly leaves and shoots, grows all around them throughout the year. They do not have to walk, run, hunt for it, or fight over it. From breakfast to suppertime they just walk slowly, upside down, from one branch to another, grasping a leaf here, a bud there, and munching quietly. Between meals they sleep. A sloth may spend its whole life in just one tree.

But the first difficulty is finding them, for no other animal has a simpler or more effective camouflage. The coarse brownish fur, the color of tree bark, grows in directions that shed rain. Each hair is grooved, and within those grooves grow green algae — the single-celled plants that also grow on bark. So the sloth matches almost exactly the tree that is its kingdom.

Arctic fox and hare LIFE IN A WHITE WORLD

The Arctic, the cold region surrounding the North Pole, is snow-covered for over half the year. When the snow disappears in summer, the tundra landscape becomes green and brown, with a brief but brilliant flush of color from thousands of tiny flowers. In autumn, much of the vegetation turns red, before disappearing under winter snow. Many of the tundra birds and mammals spend only their summers there. A few, like this Arctic hare and Arctic fox, live there all year round.

Hares live on the meager grasses and other vegetation of the tundra, feeding well in summer, but having to scratch through the snow for food in winter. Foxes live on small birds and mammals, including Arctic hares. Both benefit from being able to merge with their background. But like the background, they have to change with the seasons. In the far north, both

spend their winters in dense white coats, the fox creamy-white to match the snow in sunshine, the hare bluish-white to blend with the shadows. In spring, the fox's coat molts to a thinner brown fur, while the Arctic hares remain white. Further south, where there is less snow, the foxes remain brown throughout the year, while the hares turn mottled brown for the summer.

— Numbat MARSUPIAL WITH MATCHING STRIPES

This animal looks like a large, striped squirrel, but it is a numbat, from the eucalyptus forests of southwestern Australia. Its main food is termites, which are antlike insects that live in colonies and feed on wood. Numbats live mainly on the ground, where the termites live, but can also climb trees and scramble among branches. They are about 18 inches (45 cm) long from nose to tip of tail. Their pattern of stripes blends wonderfully with the pattern of leaves and dappled sunlight on the forest floor. When frightened by a dog or other predator, the numbat hides in a hollow log, blocking the entrance with its rump.

Like kangaroos and wombats, numbats are marsupials — mammals that give birth to very tiny live young and carry them around in a pouch for the first few weeks. The long nose hides a long row of teeth (52 altogether, more than any other land mammal) and an even longer tongue. Using its strong claws, the numbat rips holes in a termite nest or rotting log, pokes its tongue into the holes, whisks out the termites, and cracks them between those many sharp teeth.

Numbats use their long tongue
to lick up termites.

— Plaice A FISH THAT CHANGES ITS SPOTS

The shallow seabed is full of life, and consequently, full of dangers. The plaice is one of many kinds of fish that live on the gravel surface, darting here and there to pick up drifting particles of food, occasionally digging in the sand to find other scraps — perhaps worms, perhaps dead or dying shrimps or sea spiders.

Millions of years ago the ancestors of plaice were ordinary fish, with bodies shaped like herrings or salmon. They probably fed above the gravelly seabed, as other fish do today. But some found it more effective to lie down on one side and browse, and to flatten themselves against the seabed. Over the years they became flatfish, like this plaice, with the underside eye moving to the upper surface. Changes in their camouflage also occur in the everyday life of these fish. The brown skin contains tiny sacs of paintlike pigments. These can expand to show blobs of color, or contract to pinpoint size. So the plaice changes color to match its background, and is very hard to see.

Geometrid moth SAFE LANDING IN THE LITTER

There are thousands of species of moths and butterflies, all with different needs for display and camouflage. Some need to be brilliant, so that they can attract mates. Others need to be highly colored, so they blend with highly colored backgrounds such as clusters of flowers. Still others seem to benefit by blending in against dull backgrounds, perhaps because they lay their eggs there and need to match them as closely as possible. Of these less-brilliant forms, some have come to match particular backgrounds, such as tree bark or living or dead leaves. This is because butterflies and moths alike are seriously hunted by birds, lizards, and other predators. It pays for some of them at least to hide when they land, making it more difficult for a sharp-eyed predator to spot them.

Here is a moth that looks almost exactly like a dead leaf. Called the geometrid moth, it lives in rainforests. Though several kinds of leaves fall to the forest floor, this moth has adapted to match very precisely those of a particular shape and color. To hide, it just has to land among those kinds of leaves, which it seems to recognize by sight or possibly by scent.

Common toad MAGIC IN THE GARDEN

If you have a garden with a cool, damp corner, you will almost certainly have a few resident toads. Though many people thought they were magical and could work miracles, few ever thought them beautiful. The common frog looks smart and well-tailored alongside the common toad. But even the common toad can tell us something of how the world works.

Common toads are found throughout Europe, northern Africa, and Asia. There are similar species in North and South America. Small and squat, they live close to the soil, for which their rough, bumpy surface is a remarkably good match. Unlike plaice and chameleons, they cannot change color to match a particular background. But their rough, mottled, green-gray-brown skin blends with almost any natural surface in the environment in which they live. A universal, general-purpose camouflage, it clearly serves them well. If the camouflage fails, toads have other tricks to protect themselves, including glands near the eyes that produce bad-tasting poison. A dog that catches a toad will spit it out and leaves them alone in future.

Take care of the toads in your garden. They may have run short of magic, but they earn their keep by munching slugs, snails, ants, and other garden pests.

Tree frog PUZZLE: FIND THE FROG

If the common toad has a general-purpose camouflage, this little animal has one of the most effective specialized camouflages of all. It is a tree frog, and it is just a few inches long. There are about 500 species, living in warm climates all over the world. This particular one lives in the damp tropical forests of Madagascar.

We usually think of frogs as creatures that live in ponds, needing water close by all the time — especially in spring, when they lay eggs that turn into tadpoles. In warm, rainy areas, the trunk and branches of trees become covered with mosses and other small plants, which soak up and hold moisture. There are even tiny ponds, like water gardens far above the ground, with enough moisture to keep frogs damp and happy, and enough visiting insects to feed them. When it comes to breeding time, some tree frogs return to the ground to lay eggs, while others lay them in the damp mosses or tiny pools of the trees.

As a result, tree frogs have evolved that climb rather than swim, and these have flattened toes and fingers. Living as they do among predatory birds, it pays for them to match their backgrounds as closely as possible – hence the very impressive camouflage of this little frog.

Flattened fingers and toes help the
tree frog to climb, rather than swim.

Tawny frogmouth SITTING STILL FOR SAFETY

There are a dozen different kinds of frogmouths. All live in tropical forests from southern India to southeastern Asia and southern China, and in temperate forests and bushland of eastern Australia. Mostly gray-brown to black, they feed on insects. You would not guess from the main picture why these birds are called frogmouths. But, as the picture below shows, they have an enormous, wide bill with bright lining — like a yellow pocket. They feed on flying insects. Some say they hold the bill open and the insects fly in, but that is not very likely. At twilight, frogmouths flitter around like bats, picking their prey off shrubs and leaves. Some of the insects are the size of small mice, so a big bill helps.

Frogmouths feed mainly at night, when most flying insects are about, so they have to sleep during the day. That can be dangerous, because daytime is when other predators are around, looking for something to eat. So the frogmouth perches on a branch, preferably an old one with moss and twigs that match its feathers. Sitting very still and rigid, with eyes seemingly closed and bill pointing upward, it looks just like another branch.

It is not quite so fast asleep as you might think, and its eyes are not completely closed. If you approach and make a grab, it will wait till the last moment, then fly away.

The frogmouth's enormous, wide bill allows it to catch insects as big as small mice.

Tiger cat TIGER IN THE RAIN

Though called a tiger cat, this creature is neither a tiger nor a cat. It is as big as a cat, and it acts like one, especially when there is a plump robin just ahead. But we are in Tasmania, off the southern coast of Australia, and this is a native marsupial that scientists call a dasyure.

Marsupials give birth to their young while they are still very small, and carry them around for the first few weeks of life, often in a pocket or pouch. This tiger cat may well have five or six tiny kittens, only 2 inches (5 cm) long, in a pouch under its belly.

Why are they called tiger cats? Early settlers thought of them as a kind of cat, and hunted them because they killed their chickens. When cornered, they growled and spat fiercely, earning the additional name of tiger.

Tasmania gets a lot of rain, especially on its western side, and the natural vegetation is dense temperate forest. Dasyures live on the ground and in the trees, hunting for birds, lizards, and small mammals. Much of the forest has been replaced by farms and towns, but the dasyures are still around. Their brown coats, spotted with white, provide good camouflage when they are climbing among old, lichen-covered tree trunks, and keep them well hidden on the damp forest floor.

Diamondback rattlesnake

There are about 30 different kinds of rattlesnakes, and most of them live in dry or desert areas of North America. This western diamondback lives in the Mojave Desert of southern California. It gets its name from the pale, tawny diamond patterns down its back. Rattlesnakes are so-called for the curious "rattle" of dried skin on their tail, which they sound when threatened. Rattles vary a lot, but a noisy one can be heard 6 to 7 feet (2 m) away.

Rattlesnakes like dry sandy conditions, and live among thornbushes, cactus, and other desert vegetation. They hunt mainly in the evenings and at night, taking the small mammals and reptiles that emerge to feed after the heat of the day. During the day they rest, sometimes in holes or under rocks, or in whatever shade they can find. This one has found an old cactus plant, half of it dead or dying, and has curled up to rest in one of the stems. The snake's drab coloring matches the dry vegetation around it.

Why should a well-camouflaged snake need a rattle, which draws attention to it? Experts do not know for sure, but it is most probably to act as a warning, to keep other animals from treading on the snake and damaging it accidentally.

— Wild hogs PLAIN PARENTS, STRIPED YOUNG

Farm hogs that you see in sties and fields give you very little sense of what hogs are really about. Wild hogs in a forest tell you far more. The giveaway is their shape. Wild hogs are narrow at the front, broad at the shoulders, with very powerful hindquarters. That is the ideal shape for pushing through trees and dense undergrowth. The pointed snout, backed by a strong neck, is a superefficient digging tool. Hogs can effectively plow a field with their noses, looking for roots and young shoots, and riffle through leaf litter in search of fungi, acorns, or anything else that is edible.

Domestic hogs, derived from wild hogs of Europe and Asia, are mostly white, sometimes black or tan, with hair so fine that they have to be protected against sunburn. Wild hogs have darker skin, and a darker and denser covering of hair, making them far less visible either in the forest or in open grassland. Most young domestic hogs are white, too, but wild ones like those pictured below are dark tan or brown, with white, yellow, or brown stripes, which help to hide them from forest predators.

Snowy owl HUNTER OF THE ICY TUNDRA

There are about 130 different kinds of owls in the world, most of them gray or brown birds of forest and grassland. This is a snowy owl of the Arctic. Though not the largest owl, it is a hulking, solidly built bird, 2 feet (60 cm) long.

How does a predatory bird hide itself in the Arctic? By growing snow-white feathers? No, because the snow itself is seldom "snow-white." Depending on the light, and how the wind and sun have altered the snow's surface, it may be white, gray, patchy, dappled, or streaked with shadow. When the snow disappears, leaving rough grass and bare soil, an all-white bird would really stand out. Snowy owls have the answer. The face, throat, and well-feathered feet are white; the rest of the plumage is heavily barred with narrow black streaks. Its bill and claws are black. Only the vivid orange eyes provide a splash of color.

This owl has caught a lemming, a mouselike mammal that burrows in the snow and feeds on the seeds from last year's grass. It may also catch ducks, baby geese, wading birds, ground squirrels, and any other small bird or mammal. This snowy owl has made a lucky catch. Snow has been falling heavily, and that always makes hunting difficult.

Jackson's chameleon CHANGING COLOR TO ORDER

Chameleons are a family of lizards that live in warm countries from southern Spain to Africa, through the Middle East, Madagascar, India, and Sri Lanka. Ranging in length from 2 to 3 inches (8 cm) to 2 feet (60 cm), they have a rippled skin covered with bumps. Some, like this African Jackson's chameleon, have horns on the front of their head. They eat insects and spiders, which they catch at a distance by shooting out a very long tongue. When the chameleon sees an insect, it pushes the tongue forward and, by muscular pressure, shapes it suddenly into a slender tube that may be longer than its owner. Well aimed, the tip of the tongue sticks to the prey and hauls it back into the chameleon's mouth. When not extended, the tongue fits comfortably inside the chameleon's mouth.

Chameleons are said to be able to change color almost infinitely, according to their background. But this is not strictly true. Each species has a basic skin color, in this case green, which can be varied by quickly altering the size of tiny packages of color pigment under the skin surface. This gives chameleons a range of colors, including black, which they can switch unconsciously to give passable imitations of their background.

Bittern A PUZZLE FOR BIRD-WATCHERS

You are much more likely to hear bitterns than to see them. Brown, speckled birds, they have long legs and long necks, with a dark head and white throat. They have surprisingly deep, booming voices. They live on lakes, nesting among reeds by the water's edge. On a still day, their "booms" carry for miles across the water. Males boom to warn other males to keep away, and to tell females that they are looking for company.

European bitterns stand about 30 inches (75 cm) tall. American bitterns are similar but slightly smaller. Bitterns used to be common wherever there were freshwater lakes and plenty of reeds. Now that many of the lakes have been filled in and built over, there are not so many bitterns. To see one, take a rowboat or canoe — a small, quiet boat without a noisy engine — and paddle along the edge of a lake. You will find it hard to pinpoint just where the booming comes from. But if you are lucky, you will see something like this bittern that is in an alert posture, with head pointing to the sky, looking as much as possible like a bunch of reeds. It is not lost in thought. Those beady eyes, on either side of its bill, are watching you very closely.

In flight, bitterns pull back their neck like large brown owls, but the long bill is the giveaway.

Crab spider DEATH AMONG THE FLOWERS

Spiders come in all shapes and forms. This one looks like a miniature crab, with long, jointed legs curving back from its body. It even scuttles sideways like a crab. But that is not its main form of camouflage. The spider crab's trick is to be born in a wide variety of colors, and for each to find a flower of its own color to hide in. Here, in a peaceful meadow, we have a vivid yellow crab spider sitting in a flower that it matches almost exactly. The match is so good that a bee or fly visiting the flower to collect nectar will fail to see the spider altogether. When the insect comes within range, the spider grabs it, injects poison to paralyze it, then sucks out its juices.

Color matching is not quite so simple as it looks, for insects probably see colors differently than we do. The spider and flower have to match exactly, too, within the range of vision of the insect. But pink crab spiders find appropriate pink flowers, blue ones find blue flowers, and yellow ones find yellow flowers. If you move one onto a flower of the wrong color, it becomes restless and wanders off to find one that is right.

Woodcock WHEN THE TREES ARE BROWN ...

Some call this the world's most beautiful bird. About 1 foot (30 cm) long, stockily built, with a long, probing bill, it lives in Europe and in Asia as far east as China. A closely related species breeds in the eastern United States. You will not find woodcocks in busy places. They live in remote woodlands, widely scattered, each with an extensive territory that it patrols in a whirring flight. Often you see them flying over their territories in the evening.

Close up they are magical, handsome birds, richly barred in black, gold, and several shades of brown. On the nest, or just roosting, they sit very, very still, matching almost exactly a background of old leaves, twigs, and grasses. They are so well matched that you seldom see them until, almost unbelievably, one flies up from under your feet.

Female woodcocks disturbed at the nest have another trick to play. They run back and forth nearby with one wing trailing, as though injured. A person may see through the trick, but a fox or stoat might just be tempted to follow her, and be diverted away from the nest of vulnerable eggs or chicks.

45

Orchid mantis DANGEROUS BEAUTY

Here is another insect with a remarkable eye for color — .an orchid mantis of Indonesia and Malaysia, specialized for living in pink and violet orchids. Mantises are strange, leggy insects with long, slender bodies, short wings, and elaborately folding limbs. They specialize in catching and eating other insects. About 1,800 different mantises inhabit warm countries all over the world. The green praying mantis of southern Europe (so-called because it sits upright with "hands" together, as though in prayer) is perhaps the best known, but this is a dull, everyday creature compared with its tropical cousins.

There are many kinds of flower mantises that, like crab spiders, specialize in matching flowers of particular colors. Orchid mantises take the whole business of camouflage a step farther, by mimicking almost exactly, not only in color but also in shape, some of the world's most complex flowers.

This one is mimicking an orchid of rare beauty. The limbs have developed broad flanges of exactly the right shape and color. Wings, head, and abdomen have all been tinted perfectly, in delicate shades of pink and violet, to increase the illusion. So what happens now? Any insect hovering near, attracted perhaps by the orchid's heavy perfume, will be grabbed by those delicately tinted forelimbs, overpowered, and eaten.

Index CREATURES, HABITATS, AND PLACES